Spot Thompson

ALFA BEER
Discover the Hellenic spirit

This land is full of crossroads. Each one of them leads you to the most exciting experiences.
So start from the beginning.
Start with an "A". Start with a cool ALFA beer.
An authentic Hellenic taste that you can enjoy wherever you are.
Start with an ALFA beer and make the first step to a unique world full of excitement. Welcome to Hellas.

CONTENTS

CONTENTS

BEST

GREEK COOKING
REINVENTED

MARIA HARAMIS

ONLY THE BEST CREDITS

Publisher and Editor in Chief	Alexander Kyrtsis
Editor	Veti Nikolopoulou
Texts	Maria Haramis
Photographer	Thanassis Tavernarakis
Translation	Diana Farr Louis
Proofreading	Niki Potamianou
Communications Department	Faye Nikolopoulou
Advertising Department	Vicky Magoulioti
Secretariat	Georgina Karnesi
Editorial Secretary	Panagiota Georgala
Accounts Department	Costas Bistouras
	Dimitris Draïnas
Sales	George Gerokonstandis
Logistics	Dimitris Athanasopoulos
Design and Layout	Antigoni Terkas
Colour Separation	Next S.A.
Production	EPIPHANIA S.A.

Copyright (C) 2001, AXON PUBLICATIONS S.A.
First Edition: October 2001
52 Aigialias Street, 151 25 Maroussi,
Greece, tell ++30-(0)1-06856093, fax 06856095
email: axon@hol.gr
www.greeceonlythebest.gr
ISBN: 960-377-055-8

The precious oil of a blessed land SITIA O.3

The most admired and much awarded olive oil...

This oil, which is distinguished by its golden-green colour, its intricate fresh aromas of unripe fruit and green herbs, the balance between sweet and bitter, the magical taste on the tongue and the amazing duration of its after-taste, has travelled all over the world and has charmed it.

This exceptional extra virgin olive oil, SITIA 0,3, was awarded the 1st prize, in 1998, in the competition organized by the Spanish National Council of Olive Oil, in the 5th SOL Exhibition in Italy, in 1999, and in 2001 by the International Olive oil Council in France, confirming and rewarding in this way the endeavours of the Union of Agricultural Cooperatives of Sitia.

...daily verification for the mind and body...

The greatest prize of all though that SITIA O,3 has been accepted comes from the consumers themselves who, honouring the superior taste and its beneficial properties for human health, have established it in their daily diet. In addition, another advantage of SITIA O,3 is its many uses. It is an oil so delicious that it can be used "as is" in salads, with greens, fish and vegetables, in cooking and in frying because it withstands especially high temperatures.

Finally, a secret in order to preserve all the nutritious and tasty characteristics is to add the oil to food 10 minutes before finishing cooking.

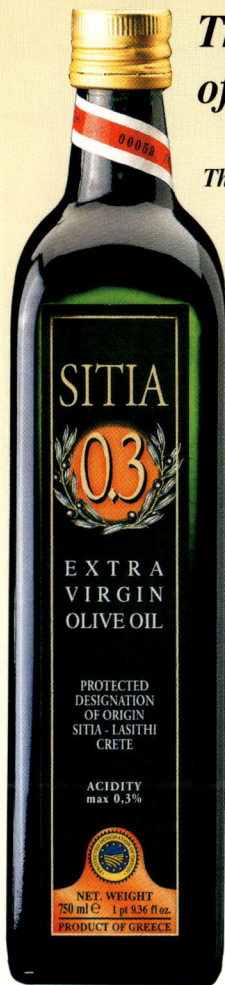

Union of agricultural cooperatives of Sitia
74, Misonos Street, GR-72300 Sitia Crete Greece
Tel.: + 30 843 22211, 22954, 23331
Fax: 0843-23222

*T*he ancient peoples of the Mediterranean have always conversed. We are united by the Sea, the noon-day Sun overhead, the transparent air. These have produced indolence, extroversion, poverty and shrewdness. The lands surrounding the Middle Sea live at rhythms that are larghetto, vivace, allegro but never moderato. Sailors, poets, and merchants trade in coin, theory, products, ploys. They borrow and lend all to each other.

Therefore the pastitsio and moussaka paternity questions - Greek or Roman, Turkish or Byzantine? - are devoid of import, scientific relevance and indeed of significance. If like causes produce like effects then the geological, climatic and cultural affinities in the region lead to similar culinary results. The few exceptions simply add spice, to which I dutifully pay my respects. However, I think it more significant that moussaka is as tasty as it is passé. Fried eggplant, browned mince-meat and béchamel constitute a threat to our arteries, waistline and silhouette. The demand for more healthy food concerns me as much as it does you.

So, in the first place this collection of recipes will ignore the sterile search for the origins of dishes. Carefree, we will saunter through the cuisines of neighbours, friends, and enemies and anthologize whatever we like. In the second place, we will lighten, condense and simplify procedures wherever possible. Furthermore, we will resurrect and eliminate the guilt from those dishes that we were brought up on but which we have turned our backs on. Chicken Milanese for example, or mocha cream with Greek coffee. In short, this little book will not sermonize. It will dance here and there, have fun, be moved, make fun of itself. It will though translate using the tools of the choicest Greek ingredients. It will speak of a cuisine based mostly on olive oil, which does not use flour to thicken sauces but depends on the home-made broths which are one of the fundamental tricks of great chefs. When using my, or others', recipes experiment with using the broth of vegetables, fish, mushrooms, chickens or crayfish instead of water and you won't regret it.

THE CHOICEST INGREDIENT

The great chefs we were talking about are those honoured with three Michelin stars, given 19 out of 20 by Gault-Millen, praised by Zagat, that new American institution, and singled out by the most reputable food-critics.

During my career as a journalist I have interviewed, known and eaten with most of the great chefs who have interested me.

4

All but one, the intellectual Conticini, agreed on one point: that at least seventy percent of the success of a dish depends on the quality of the ingredients. I would raise that percentage to 85, but we don't admit it, preferring to have people think our skill is more important. In reality, as Alain Ducasse said to me, the chef's chief talent lies in finding and discovering fine and rare ingredients.

And I believe him. All the following recipes have been tried, tested and photographed. We cooked with chef Grigoris Bithikiotis, using first-rate Greek products and produce. Those I esteem and am proud of, which I have in my pantry and cellar, which I know how they are made or which I arrived at after experimentation.

Make pastry with commercial flour and then with good, yellow, living flour from a water-mill. The first pie will not bear comparison with the second. The same applies to country eggs and chickens against their supermarket imitations.

I sing the praises of Aegina pistachios, Volos and Trizinia almonds, Peloponnesus highland walnuts and Mount Athos hazelnuts such as we read about in *Elytis's poem* Axion Esti. I sing the praises of Chios mastic and Taygetos oregano. Of Nevrokopi beans and the 'dry' vegetables of the islands. Oh, those unwatered eggplants and tomatoes of Santorini. Also Zaharo tomatoes, Olympus and Edessa cherries, peaches in lemon sauce and royal figs from Kymi. I give thanks for the wild mushrooms of the mountains of Epirus and the islands, for the *lagordi*, the white truffle of Santorini, for the scallops and sweet anchovies of Lesbos, for the lobsters of Astypalea, the parrot-fish of Crete, the red mullets of the Saronic Gulf and for the ever-present *marida* or white bait. Not to forget the big grey mullets and the eels of Mesolongi, the preserved fish-roe of my friend Zafeiris Trikalinos, the cigale de mer, and the baby squid which are so delicious it is considered hubris to fry them. I have cooked lean island kid and fat baby lamb.

I have studiously avoided beef for obvious reasons, but I have found country pork and friends have provided game. I have made ice cream with milk from an Attica farm and sorbets with blood oranges from Aigio and roses cut from the gardens of the northern suburbs of Athens. Vasilis Paparounas, proprietor of the much loved Symposio restaurant in Athens, provided me with butter made from sheep and goat milk from his own animals in the Pindos mountains. As the granddaughter of a pastry-cook, I believe that sweets in general are better with butter than with oil.

UNION OF VINICULTURAL **U.V.C.S.** CO-OPERATIVES OF SAMOS

Samos muscat.
The wine that conquered
the world.

DESSERT WINES

SOLID

DRY WHITE MUSCAT WINES

UNION OF VINICULTURAL CO-OPERATIVES OF SAMOS
Malagari, 83 100 SAMOS, TEL.: (0273) 27 458, 27 381, 22 572, FAX: (0273) 23 907, e-mail: info@samoswine.gr website: www.samoswine.gr

INTRODUCTION

EXTRA VIRGIN OLIVE OIL

Speaking of oil, it is an axiom that everybody prefers the oil of their own home town or village. People understandably seek out the flavours they grew up with. The matter is complicated by the fact that people consider that which they like to be good. However, what is familiar is not necessary what is better. I myself was brought up with the oils of Laconia, Messinia and Ilia, all Peloponnesian oils. The oil of Mytilini seems thin to me and acidic, since they allow the olives to fall to the ground and become damaged before pressing. Cretan oils seemed too heavy up until about ten years ago. They have improved no end and those of the Sitia co-operatives especially have finally earned my loyalty. And not just mine. That would not be enough. The Paris based International Olive Oil Council awarded its coveted gold medal to Sitia Extra Virgin Olive Oil on June 13, 2001. Their new label proudly proclaims a maximum acidity of 0.3%. This fabulous oil is pressed from a single variety of olives, Koroneiki, which grows primarily in the highlands and well drained areas.

But what are the tell-tale features of good olive oil? How are you the consumer going to distinguish between all those brands out there? The colour should range from green to gold and be vivid. Yellow is less desirable. The odour should remind you of crushed olives. That is what is meant by 'fruity' in olive oil. A secondary odour becomes perceptible on the palate. With a small sip of the oil, inhale some air and mix the two in your mouth. The taste will be bitter or you might feel a sting in the back of your throat. These are good. If however the taste is metallic or mouldy, this is not. Also undesirable is an unpleasant feeling of greasiness on the palate which connotes high acidity. Did you like the lesson?

WHAT ABOUT WINE?

Fortunately, the wine flows without cease. The world of wine-tasting is endless. It demands constant perspicuity, updating, trials. Every year constitutes a new point of departure for every one of a wine producer's labels. A new vintage initiates a new cycle of experiences, hopes, disappointments. For this reason, besides testing the wines, we who write about them are continually testing the criteria and our own powers. What I celebrate more than anything in my wonderful profession lies in the improvement of Greek wines with every year. The repertory, which is always being enriched, our notes, memories and references make us more experienced and better as we get older. As a practical sequence for you, the reader, don't put your faith in neophytes over mature food and wine writers.

I never thought of myself as an enlightened wine critic. I was never too embarrassed to express my preferences. I never feared disputes, though I never seek them. "Create in me a clean heart, oh God; and renew in me a right spirit", as David wrote in the 50st Psalm.

White wine I drink with a pistol pointed at my head. In other words, only when there isn't a drop of red to be found. Red wine, then, is my passion; I declare it openly. But this does not prevent me from protesting against the way we in Greece drink our red wines too young, too raw, too rough. Bottles that should be stored in the vintner's cellars for five, eight, ten years appear on the market and in restaurants when they are only 16 or 18 months old. And grate against our palate.

I have far fewer objections and a particular weakness for dessert wines. Sunshine, climate, centuries' old tradition, know-how all make the sweet wines of this country far better than their dry cousins. Nine years ago, I decided to start a crusade for Greek vins de liqueurs. Hostesses and restaurants were barely aware of Samos doux and Mavrodaphne. With some colleague friends we held informal tasting sessions and got to know the varieties available at the time. We then persuaded wine producers to bring out sweet wines alongside their range of reds, whites and rosés. And we've seen the response. By now many, many restaurants serve dessert wines. During this time and watching these developments, I am happy to note that the Samos co-operative has held high the banner of quality and deserves congratulations for keeping its products uniformly excellent.

In the beginning was the vine. On the eastern Aegean island of Pythagoras the small white muscat grape has been cultivated for thousands of years. The oldest and finest of the four muscat varietals was born in Greece. It bears a round grape with a highly concentrated taste. And it owes its name to this predominant, exuberant aroma. Our forefathers believed it reminded them of musk. Today we find in it scents of orange blossom, spices, grape of course, exotic or dried fruits, and honey.

Twenty-two villages form a natural amphitheatre of vineyards, and the vines are often planted on terraces held together by dry-stone walls at altitudes of up to 800 metres. Low temperatures, a great deal of sunshine, a prevalence of schist and gravel in the soil promoting good drainage combine to create exceptional conditions for the production of good wine. The result: in the demanding French market, the dessert wines of Samos are the leading imports. I am pleased to be an ambassadress of our muscat wines and I recommend them to you without reservation, especially because the value for money makes them such a steal.

For more information about Greek wines, why not order a copy of the superb **BEST Guide to Greek Wines**, by calling 010 6856093.

FESTIVE BREAD

for 2 loaves

- *9 grams dry yeast or 30 grams fresh yeast*
- *1 sugar cube*
- *500 grams flour, approximately*
- *30 grams butter plus a little more for the pans, at room temperature*
- *salt*
- *a little crushed mastic**
- *2 pinches mahlepi**, optional*
- *1 vanilla bean*
- *handful of browned sesame seeds, optional*

Dissolve the brewer's yeast and the sugar cube in a little tepid water, pour it into the mixer bowl, add 100 grams of flour and stir with a wooden spoon. Leave undisturbed in a warm place for 30-45 minutes to rise.

Add the butter, mixing well for it to melt. Add the flour, the aromatics, a pinch of salt, and beat in the mixer, adding a little water until the dough becomes elastic. With the pastry hook, continue to beat for about 12-18 minutes at medium speed. Cover the bowl with a clean linen cloth and leave it in a warm spot for the dough to rise for 3 hours or in the refrigerator overnight.

Preheat the oven to 190 °C.

Lift the dough out of the bowl and knead it a bit with wet hands. Divide it into two balls.

Butter two bread pans, dust with a little flour, shaking the pan to remove excess flour. Shape the dough balls into loaves and arrange in the pans. Sprinkle with sesame seeds if desired.

Set the bread pans on the stove, which will be warm from the oven, and leave them there for 15-20 minutes.

Bake for 10 minutes on the floor of the oven. Lower the temperature to 180 °C and bake for 30-40 minutes on the middle rack until the bread becomes an appetizing colour. Remove the pans from the oven and immediately remove the bread to wire racks to cool.

* see note on page 123
** a Turkish spice, to be found at Greek and Middle Eastern grocers.

SAFFRON MAYONNAISE

- *1/4 teaspoon powdered saffron*
- *3 egg yolks*
- *1 tablespoon powdered mustard*
- *200 ml sunflower or sesame seed oil*
- *100 ml extra virgin olive oil*
- *juice of 1/2 small lemon*
- *salt, freshly ground white pepper*
- *1 tablespoon white wine vinegar*

Dissolve the saffron in 1 1/2 tablespoons hot water, cover and let cool.

Place the egg yolks, mustard and salt in the bowl of your mixer and blend well. Add a few drops of seed oil and blend for 45 seconds or until you have an emulsion. Continue beating in a few drops of oil at a time, waiting until they are absorbed before proceeding with the next dose. Add a little more oil as the mixture thickens and increase the speed of the mixer until the mayonnaise is pale and silken in texture. When all the seed oil has been used, add the olive oil in the same way, followed by the lemon juice. Add the pepper and vinegar, beat a bit more, and finally beat in the saffron. Goes well with steamed fish and vegetables.

RUBY GARLIC SAUCE

- *1 1/2 kilos beetroot with greens*
- *4-5 garlic cloves, green shoots removed*
- *350 grams boiling potatoes*
- *60 grams walnuts, finely chopped*
- *extra virgin olive oil*
- *1-2 tablespoons white wine vinegar*
- *salt, freshly ground pepper*

Preheat the oven to 150 °C. Cut off the beet greens, wash well and drain in a colander. Scrub the beetroot with a wire sponge under the tap, removing any blemishes or rough skin. Dry and rub each beetroot with oil. Line a baking dish with a few of the beet leaves, place the beetroots on top of them, sprinkle with salt and bake for 20 minutes. Cover the dish with a piece of aluminium foil and bake for another 30 minutes or until the beets root are fork tender.

When the beetroot are cool enough to handle, remove the skin and cut them into large cubes or slices about 1/2 cm thick.

Boil the remaining beet greens in plenty of salted water. Drain, reserving the liquid which will be a deep pink. Dry the leaves, line a platter with half of them, finely chop the other half and mix them with the beetroot cubes.

Wash and scrub the potatoes under the tap and boil them in the pink beet liquid, adding salt if necessary. When they are soft and just cool enough to handle, peel them. Mash the garlic with a little salt in the mortar or mixer. Add the hot potatoes one at a time to the mixing bowl, trickling in olive oil a few drops at a time as if you were making mayonnaise, continuing to beat or pound with the pestle all the while. Add 30 grams of the walnuts and pepper. If you want to deepen the colour of the purée, add some beetroot cubes.

In a separate bowl, dissolve a little salt in the vinegar, add 4 tablespoons of oil and the rest of the walnuts. Stir vigorously and pour the dressing over the beetroot. Put the garlic sauce into a bowl and serve separately.

MY GRANDMOTHER'S TARAMOSALATA

This is a favourite Lenten speciality which is usually eaten with warm fresh bread or even boiled fish. You can also make it in a food processor.

8 servings

- 500 grams boiling potatoes of equal size
- 40 grams white tarama paste
- extra virgin olive oil
- juice of 1/2 small lemon
- 1-2 tablespoons white wine vinegar
- freshly ground pepper

Wash the potatoes under the tap and scrub with a wire sponge. Boil them in 1 1/2-2 cups of water until tender, adding more water if necessary. Peel the potatoes while they are still hot and purée them in a mixer or potato sieve.

Pound the tarama paste in a mortar with 2 tablespoons of oil and add the potatoes gradually until you have a smooth amalgam. Add a little more oil, a few drops of lemon juice, a few drops of vinegar, a bit more oil, lemon and vinegar, and continue in this way until the taramosalata becomes light and fluffy. Taste for seasonings and sprinkle with black pepper.

Tarama paste is pressed carp roe. The so-called white tarama has less salt, a more delicate flavour and no artificial colouring, as opposed to the more common red paste.

TZATZIKI WITH A DIFFERENCE

What visitor to Greece hasn't tasted this refreshing dip, which is usually loaded with garlic. Here the effect is more spicy and crunchy.

4 servings

- *2 medium cucumbers*
- *coarse salt*
- *400 ml Greek strained yogurt*
- *a handful of finely chopped mint*
- *2 tablespoons sesame seeds, toasted in the frying pan*
- *sweet paprika and cayenne pepper*

Peel the cucumbers and chop into tiny dice. Sprinkle with coarse salt and drain in a colander for 30 minutes. Rinse off the salt.

Dry the cucumber cubes and mix them in a bowl with the yogurt and other ingredients. Cover the bowl with cling film and refrigerate for 2 hours before serving.

SKORDALIA - GARLIC SAUCE WITH PISTACHIOS

A cross between mayonnaise and mashed potatoes, skordalia goes beautifully with steamed vegetables and white-fleshed fish.

- *8 cloves garlic*
- *extra virgin olive oil*
- *sea salt*
- *500 grams boiling potatoes*
- *150 grams pistachios, shelled and finely chopped*
- *6 tablespoons lemon juice*

Preheat the oven to 120 °C. Peel the garlic, except for the final layer. Place the cloves on a piece of aluminium foil, sprinkle with oil, fold the foil into a packet and roast in the oven for at least 1 hour. Squeeze out the soft garlic into a mortar or mixing bowl, add a pinch of salt and pound with the pestle or a wooden spoon until smooth. Peel the potatoes and boil until soft in a little salted water. Add the potatoes one by one to the mortar and mash them with the garlic. (If you don't have a mortar and pestle, a potato sieve will do.) Gradually mix in the pistachios and start adding the oil, a tablespoon at a time, always stirring in the same direction. When the mixture has absorbed 4-5 tablespoons of oil, slowly pour in the lemon juice and the rest of the oil, in alternation, until the sauce has become smooth, viscous and somewhat gummy.

"*F*AKE" EASTER SOUP

The egg-lemon flavoured soup eaten after the midnight service on Easter Eve is usually made with lamb innards.

6 servings

* 700 grams wild mushrooms of various types or a mixture of cultivated mushrooms
* olive oil
* 1 medium onion, grated
* 6 spring onions, finely chopped
* 1 1/2 litres chicken, vegetable or mushroom broth
* finely chopped dill
* 2 eggs
* juice of 1 1/2 lemons
* salt, freshly ground pepper

Wash the mushrooms, cut off the tough stems if necessary, cut the larger ones into two or three, and drain. Gently heat 4-5 tablespoons of olive oil in a deep saucepan and sauté the onion until it is translucent. Add the spring onions and sauté for another 3 minutes. Add the mushrooms, stir and brown for 3-4 minutes. Add the broth, dill, salt and pepper and bring to a boil. Simmer for 25 minutes.

Beat the eggs with 2 tablespoons of oil and season with salt and pepper to taste. Add 2 tablespoons of broth to the eggs, beating constantly. Add the lemon juice and continue beating.

Remove the pot with the mushrooms from the stove, add a few tablespoons of broth to the egg-lemon sauce, stirring all the while, and then pour the sauce into the pot. Shake and stir, heat very gently and serve.

*M*Y TPAHANA WITH CHESTNUTS

4 servings

- *500 grams boiling chestnuts*
- *110 grams butter*
- *1 medium leek, finely chopped*
- *180 grams trahana*
- *salt, cayenne pepper and freshly ground black pepper*

*W*ith a sharp knife make 3 slits in each chestnut. Boil them in salted water for 30 minutes. Drain and remove the hard shells and soft inner skin.

Melt 40 grams of butter in a frying pan and brown the chestnuts over medium heat for 3-4 minutes. Remove and set them in a low oven to keep warm. Heat the remaining butter and sauté the leek until it is soft. Add the trahana to the saucepan and sauté, stirring, for 2 minutes. Add 2 litres of water, salt, lower the heat and simmer, stirring from time to time, for 10-15 minutes until the trahana is soft and the soup is thick.

Add the chestnuts, stir, boil for another 2 minutes, season with the cayenne and pepper and serve.

Trahana is a staple throughout the Balkans and Turkey. It is made with ground wheat and fresh or sour milk and has a pleasant tangy taste. It can be eaten on its own as a sort of porridge or added to meat or vegetable soups for extra thickening and flavour. It can be found in health food shops or ethnic markets. If you cannot find it, use bulgur instead.

*S*PRING ARTICHOKES

6 servings

- *12 small artichokes*
- *3 lemons*
- *250 grams fresh peas*
- *250 grams baby carrots*
- *350 grams small new potatoes*
- *8 tablespoons extra virgin olive oil*
- *4 spring onions, finely chopped*
- *1 cup fennel leaves, finely chopped*
- *salt and freshly ground pepper*

Remove the tough outer leaves and the choke from the artichokes, cut off the stalks and trim the bottoms, leaving just a tiny point of peeled stalk. Place the artichokes in a bowl with the juice of one lemon and the rind of the other two.

Boil the stalks in a litre of salted water for 15 minutes. Strain, reserving the liquid, and discard the stalks.

Shell the peas. Trim the ends off the carrots and scrub or peel them, leaving them whole if they are small enough. Peel the potatoes but leave them whole, too. Heat the oil gently and saute the onions until they wilt. Add the carrots, fennel leaves, and 2 cups of liquid from the artichoke stalks, cover, and boil for 10 minutes. Add the remaining liquid, the juice of the two lemons, and bring to a boil. Add the potatoes, place the artichokes on top of them, with their bottoms pointing up, the peas, salt and pepper. Lower the heat and cover the vegetables with a piece of grease-proof paper the size of the pan. Make slits in the paper with a sharp knife and simmer without a lid for about 15 or 20 minutes, until the artichokes and potatoes are fork tender.

ARTICHOKE OMELETTE

4 servings

- *8 frozen artichokes, defrosted*
- *juice of 1/2 lemon*
- *3 eggs*
- *8 tablespoons extra virgin olive oil*
- *salt and freshly ground pepper*

Boil the artichokes in 2 1/2 cups of salted water together with the lemon juice for 12-15 minutes. Drain.
Turn on the grill.
Toss the artichokes in 4 tablespoons of oil, sprinkle them with salt and pepper and roast them under the grill for 5 minutes until they brown a little. Beat the eggs with 3 tablespoons of water and salt and pepper. Heat the remaining olive oil in a nonstick frying pan, lay the artichokes in the pan and pour the eggs over them. Fry until the omelette puffs up and turns golden.

EGGS WITH WILD ASPARAGUS

4 servings

- *800 grams wild asparagus (or cultivated, if unavailable)*
- *a pinch of baking soda*
- *extra virgin olive oil*
- *8 eggs, separated*
- *sesame seed oil*
- *2 tablespoons tangerine juice plus a little grated peel*
- *salt, freshly ground pepper*

Wash the asparagus and cut the tough ends off the stems. Tie the tips in a bundle with kitchen string. Boil the ends in salted water for 10 minutes, drain, and discard the stalks, reserving the liquid. Add the soda and boil the bundle of asparagus tips for 3-5 minutes. Drain, dry, and arrange them in a fan-shape on a round platter.

Heat a little olive oil in a non-stick frying pan. Beat the yolks lightly, add salt and pepper, and fry. Heat a little sesame seed oil in another pan. Beat the whites lightly with salt and pepper and fry separately.

Spread the egg whites in the centre of the platter and place spoonfuls of the fried yolks in little mounds on top of them.

Dissolve a little salt in the tangerine juice, add 4 tablespoons of olive oil, beat briskly with a fork and pour over the asparagus.

Sprinkle with the tangerine peel and plenty of coarsely ground pepper.

TIP
Boiling the asparagus in the broth from their stalks adds an extra element of flavour. This is a trick to use when boiling other vegetables and meats, as well.

*B*ABY CARROTS WITH CUMIN AND FETA CHEESE

4-6 servings

* *800 grams baby carrots*
* *4 bay leaves*
* *2 tablespoons cumin*
* *5 tablespoons olive oil*
* *1 medium onion, grated*
* *1/4 teaspoon sugar*
* *60-70 grams sharp feta, cubed*
* *salt, freshly ground pepper*

*W*ash the carrots, trim the tips, rub or peel if necessary. Cut 500 grams into thin sticks and leave the rest whole.

Boil the whole carrots in 2 cups of salted water seasoned with 2 bay leaves. Drain, save the carrots for another use, and reserve the broth. Gently heat the cumin in a non-stick frying pan until it browns and releases its aroma.

Gently heat the oil in an cast-iron saucepan and brown the onion until it starts to caramelize. Add the carrot sticks, the 2 bay leaves (crumbled), the cumin, salt and pepper, and sauté for 4-5 minutes. Add the sugar, stir until it dissolves, add a cup of carrot broth and simmer for 12-15 minutes, stirring once or twice, until the carrots absorb the broth and only the oil remains. Let cool in the serving dish, sprinkle with the cheese cubes and lots of coarsely ground pepper.

ℬAKED POTATO SKINS WITH BOTARGO

Botargo (avgotaraho) is pressed grey mullet roe. It is usually sold encased in yellow bee's wax and commands a higher price than almost any other delicacy except genuine Beluga and Sevruga caviar. The best avgotaraho is said to come from Mesolonghi.

4 servings

- *60 grams botargo, cleaned*
- *4 large baking potatoes (Naxos, Idaho, etc), about 200 grams each*
- *150 ml sesame seed or other oil*
- *30 grams sesame seeds*
- *juice of 1/2 lemon*
- *salt, freshly ground pepper*

ℛreheat the oven to 180 °C. Cut the fish roe into thin slices. Scrape clean the surface of each potato with a wire sponge under running water. Dry and with a fork poke several holes in each potato. Place the potatoes on a rack in the oven and bake for 1 hour. Cut each potato in half and with a spoon scoop out about half of the meat. Cut each half into strips about 2.5 cm wide.

Heat the oil in a deep fryer and fry the skins until they are golden and crisp.

Brown the sesame seeds in a non-stick frying pan until they are golden brown and start to pop.

Arrange the skins on a serving platter, sprinkle liberally with pepper, place a slice of botargo on each one, sprinkle with a drop of lemon juice, add more pepper and the browned sesame seeds and serve immediately.

*P*OTATOES BAKED WITH CUMIN

6 servings

- *1,200 grams small new potatoes*
- *4 tablespoons cumin*
- *6 tablespoons olive oil*
- *salt, freshly ground pepper*

*W*ash and scrub the potatoes with a wire sponge under the tap, dry them and cut them in half lengthwise. Spread half the potatoes on the oven rack, skin side up and grill for 15 minutes. Remove the rack, turn over the potatoes, score the cut side with a sharp knife and grill for another 15 minutes.

Brown the cumin in a non-stick frying pan over medium-high heat until it releases its aroma. Add the olive oil and heat for another minute or two. Season the potatoes with salt and pepper, pour the cumin-scented oil over them and serve.

GREEN PEPPERS STUFFED WITH TRAHANA

4 servings

- *8 green peppers*
- *400 grams ripe tomatoes*
- *280 grams onion, grated*
- *olive oil*
- *100 grams sweet trahana**
- *30 grams pine nuts (pignolias)*
- *40 grams fresh mint, finely chopped*
- *30 grams black currants, rinced*
- *30 grams parsley, finely chopped*
- *sweet paprika and cayenne pepper*
- *salt and freshly ground black pepper*

Preheat the oven to 180 °C. Rinse the peppers under the tap, slice off the top, reserving the cap with its stem, remove the seeds and white membrane inside.

Peel and de-seed the tomatoes. Cut 2 tomatoes into dice, reserving their juice. Chop the remaining tomatoes and drain them in a fine colander, reserving their juice.

Place the grated onion in a non-stick frying pan, add salt and 1/2 cup of water and simmer over medium heat until the water evaporates or is absorbed. Add 4-5 tablespoons olive oil, lower the heat and brown the onion for 5-7 minutes. Add the trahana, stir and sauté for 3 minutes. Add the pine nuts and mint and sauté, stirring, for 2 minutes. Stir in the currants, parsley, paprika, cayenne and black pepper, and cook for another 2 minutes. Add the tomato cubes and a little juice and bring to a boil. Oil a baking dish. Spoon this mixture into the peppers until they are 2/3 full - the stuffing will swell. Moisten each pepper with 1 1/2 tablespoons of tomato juice and put back its cap. Arrange the peppers in the baking dish and bake for 30-40 minutes or until the peppers are tender.

* see note page 27

COURGETTE RISSOLES

6 servings

- *500 grams medium courgettes*
- *3 eggs, beaten*
- *3 tablespoons flour*
- *1 medium leek, finely chopped*
- *mint, finely chopped*
- *basil, finely chopped*
- *1 chilli pepper, finely chopped*
- *olive oil for frying*
- *coarse and fine salt, freshly ground pepper*
- *6 little goat cheeses*

Wash the courgettes, cut off the ends and grate them coarsely. Place 1/4 of the grated courgettes in the colander, sprinkle with coarse salt, place the next 1/4, salt and so forth until all the courgettes have been salted. Let the courgettes drain in the colander for at least 4 hours. With your hands, press the water out of the courgettes, rinse off the salt well, drain again and put the grated vegetables in a clean tea towel. Squeeze tight to remove as much water as possible.

Mix the courgettes in a bowl with the eggs, flour, leek, and seasonings. Shape into 6 flattened balls.

Fry the balls in 4 tablespoons of hot oil, browning the bottom and watching the top contract. When the bottoms are a lovely golden colour, remove from the pan with a slotted spoon, add 2-3 more tablespoons of oil, heat to smoking and fry the other side of the patties. Divide the patties among 6 plates and serve with the goat cheese.

$\mathcal{M}$Y AUBERGINES WITH CELERY

6 servings

- *6 medium round aubergines*
- *4 tablespoons olive oil plus a little more*
- *1 clove garlic, finely chopped, green shoot removed,*
- *1 kilo ripe tomatoes, peeled, seeded and chopped*
- *2 branches celery, finely chopped*
- *1 sugar cube*
- *1 cinnamon stick*
- *30 grams black currants*
- *50 grams pine nuts (pignolias)*
- *salt, freshly ground pepper*

$\mathcal{P}$reheat the oven to 200 °C. Cut the aubergines into 2 - centimetre cubes. Spread the aubergine cubes in a non-stick baking dish, sprinkle with a little olive oil, salt and pepper, and bake for a few minutes until they are soft.

Brown the garlic in 4 tablespoons of olive oil for 30 seconds. Add the tomatoes, celery, sugar, cinnamon, salt and pepper, and simmer the sauce for 35-40 minutes until it thickens. Stir in the currants.

Brown the pine nuts in a non-stick frying pan until they are a deep gold. Arrange the aubergines in a deep glass serving dish, pour the tomato sauce over them, sprinkle with the pine nuts and refrigerate overnight.

ELBOW MACARONI WITH BROCCOLI

6 servings

- *2 medium heads of broccoli*
- *60 grams walnuts, coarsely chopped*
- *500 grams elbow macaroni*
- *3 tablespoons olive oil*
- *20 grams anchovy fillets*
- *2 garlic cloves, chopped, green shoots removed*
- *coarse salt, freshly ground pepper*

Wash the broccoli, peel the stalks, and coarsely chop the stalks and tips. If you wish, place them in a bowl with water acidulated with a little vinegar.

Heat a small non-stick frying pan to smoking and brown the chopped nuts, stirring with a wooden spoon until they release their oils. Remove the walnuts an set aside. Bring 5 litres of salted water to a boil, add the broccoli and parboil for 1 minute. Add the macaroni, stir and boil for a few more minutes, according to package directions.

Gently heat 3 tablespoons of oil in the same small pan. Add the anchovies, mash them with a wooden spoon, add the garlic and sauté for 1 minute. Add the walnuts, stir, and pour 1/3 of this sauce onto the serving dish.

Drain the macaroni-broccoli in a colander but save a little of the boiling water. Put on the serving dish, add the remaining sauce, thinned with the water if necessary, sprinkle with a little freshly ground pepper and serve.

$\mathscr{S}$PAGHETTI WITH BOTARGO

4 servings

- *600 grams spaghetti*
- *100 grams botargo**
- *extra virgin olive oil*
- *350 grams leeks, finely chopped*
- *juice and grated rind of 1/2 lemon*
- *salt, freshly ground pepper*

$\mathscr{B}$oil the pasta in 5 litres of bubbling water with 3 tablespoons of salt according to package directions.

Sauté the leeks in 4 tablespoons of oil over moderate heat for 8-10 minutes or until they are soft. Season to taste with salt and pepper. Cut the botargo in thin, almost transparent slices and mix with the lemon juice and 4 tablespoons of oil.

Drain the spaghetti, stir in the leeks, add the botargo and mix thoroughly. Sprinkle with the lemon peel and lots of freshly ground pepper. Serve immediately.

* See note on page 37.

EGG NOODLES WITH GOAT CHEESE

Greek egg noodles (hilopittes) are usually cut into tiny squares, but any fine long noodles will do.

4 servings

- *400 grams egg noodles*
- *70 grams or goat ewe's butter*
- *120 grams grated goat cheese*
- *salt, freshly ground pepper*

Boil the noodles according to package directions in 4 litres of salted water.

Melt the butter until it is barely browned.

Scatter 2-3 tablespoons of grated cheese on the bottom of a deep platter.

Drain the noodles, arrange on the platter, pour the melted butter over them, sprinkle with the remaining cheese and lots of pepper.

Toss and serve.

PAN-FRIED SCALLOPS AND CLAMS

4 servings

- *1 1/2 kilos scallops and hard-shell clams*
- *250 ml dry white wine*
- *100 ml sweet Samos wine or sherry*
- *3 chillis, finely chopped*
- *salt*
- *fresh oregano or parsley for garnish*

Wash and scrub the shellfish under the tap. Heat a large non-stick frying pan to burning and add the shellfish in two instalments. Lower the heat as soon as the shells open and discard any that remain closed. Simmer for 1-2 minutes. With a slotted spoon remove the shellfish into a deep serving dish.

Strain the broth from the shellfish through a coffee filter, pouring the contents into a small saucepan. Add the wines, chillis, and salt to taste. Boil vigorously to reduce by half and pour the sauce over the shellfish. Serve decorated with branches of fresh oregano.

KAKAVIA
FISHERMAN'S FISH SOUP

8 servings

- *1 grouper or other firm white "boiling" fish, about 1 kilo*
- *1 kilo rock fish*
- *1/2 kilo small shrimp*
- *2 small onions, grated*
- *350 grams carrots, halved*
- *juice of 1 large lemon*
- *2 bay leaves*
- *olive oil*
- *3 chilli peppers*
- *1/4 teaspoon saffron*
- *salt, freshly ground white pepper*

Clean and salt the fish. Boil the onions and carrots in 3 litres of salted water for 20 minutes. Let cool. Add the rock fish, bring slowly to a boil over low heat, and skim off the froth from time to time. Once it has come to the boil, simmer for 35 minutes.

Remove the fish from the saucepan, remove the large bones and mash the flesh and heads in a food mill or with a wooden spoon in a colander. Set aside the pulp.

Now add the large fish, cut in two pieces, the head, the shrimps, bay leaves and as much olive oil as you like (up to 1 cup) to the fish broth and boil vigorously, covered, for 15 minutes.

Test the fish with a fork, add the seasonings, lemon juice and rockfish pulp and boil for another 2-4 minutes.

Off the heat, remove the large fish to a platter, debone it and serve separately. Remove the head from the pan, pick off any meat, and add it to the soup.

Remove the shrimps, mash them in the food mill, and return the pulp to the soup.

Serve immediately in your best soup tureen with toasted country bread.

*S*QUID WITH SPINACH

6 servings

- *800 grams spinach*
- *1,300 grams fresh squid*
- *olive oil*
- *2 chilli peppers*
- *1 onion, grated*
- *2 medium ripe tomatoes, peeled and sliced*
- *salt, freshly ground pepper*

Clean, wash and finely slice the spinach, rolling up several leaves at a time. Parboil the spinach for a few minutes in boiling water, drain in a colander. When cool enough to handle, squeeze out as much liquid as you can. Sprinkle with salt and press the spinach against the sides of the colander with a wooden spoon. Let drain while you prepare the squid.

Clean the squid, rinse and drain. Heat 4 tablespoons of oil in a non-stick frying pan and brown the squid with the chilli peppers for 5 minutes, shaking the pan from the handle and stirring with a wooden spoon.

Gently heat 3 tablespoons of olive oil in an cast-iron saucepan and brown the onion for 5-7 minutes. Add the spinach, stirring, and sauté for 5-6 minutes. Remove the spinach from the pan and place it in the frying pan with the squid. Add the tomatoes, mix well, taste, add salt and pepper and simmer for 15-18 minutes.

MARINATED SQUID

6 servings

- *800-1,000 grams fresh squid*
- *extra virgin olive oil*
- *2 cloves garlic, green shoots removed, crushed*
- *2 chilli peppers, finely chopped*
- *grated rind of 1 orange*
- *2 cloves*
- *200 ml sweet Samos wine or sherry*
- *salt*

Wash the squid, remove the ink sacs and cartilege and cut the head off just below the eyes. Discard the head but save the tentacles. Pull off the wings and slice the body into rings.

Prepare the marinade with 4-6 tablespoons olive oil, the garlic, chillis, the orange rind and cloves. Pour the marinade over the squid and mix the ingredients well with your hands. Let stand for at least 2 hours or up to 24 hours refrigerated.

Heat a non-stick frying pan until very hot and then add 2-4 tablespoons of olive oil. Remove the squid from the marinade and slide into the oil. Fry for 3-4 minutes, stirring with a wooden spoon. Pour in the wine, stirring all the while, and add the rest of the marinade. Lower the heat, cover the pan and simmer for 8-10 minutes. The sweet wine should create a caramelized crust on the bottom of the pan. Stir, test for seasonings, add 2-3 tablespoons extra virgin olive oil and serve.

SQUID WITH FENNEL

6 servings

- *1 1/2 kilos squid*
- *500 grams bulb fennel*
- *olive oil*
- *1 medium onion, grated*
- *6 tablespoons sweet Samos wine or sherry*
- *salt, freshly ground pepper*

Wash and clean the squid, remove the transparent cartilege and cut the body in rings. Place in a colander to drain. Remove the outer layer and base of the fennel and cut in dice or narrow strips. Gently heat 3 tablespoons of olive oil in a heavy cast-iron saucepan and brown the onion for 7-8 minutes.

Heat 5 tablespoons olive oil to bubbling in a non-stick frying pan and brown the squid for 4-5 minutes, shaking the pan or stirring with a wooden spoon. Add the salt and pepper, onion and fennel, stir and sauté for 2-3 minutes. Pour in the wine, stir, lower the heat, add 125 ml/1/2 cup of water, cover, and simmer until the fennel is soft, about 8-10 minutes.

QUICK AND EASY OCTOPUS

6 servings

- *2 small octopuses, about 400-500 grams each*
- *5-6 peppercorns*
- *2 bay leaves*
- *4-5 tablespoons extra virgin olive oil*

Rinse the octopuses. Cut out the eyes, beak, and the ink sacs, which you may wish to freeze for some other use.

Heat a deep non-stick saucepan over high heat and thrown in the octopuses, cover, and reduce the heat. They will start to exude liquid. Add the bay leaves and peppercorns and continue to simmer until the liquid has been reabsorbed and the meat is tender. By now they will have acquired an appetizing reddish-brown colour, and a mouth-watering aroma will have permeated the house. Add a little olive oil, simmer over the lowest possible heat for 3 minutes, cut into bite-sized pieces and serve. This dish is also good the next day at room temperature.

TIP

For this recipe to succeed the octopus should be very fresh and the oil of the highest quality.

*S*UNBURST OF BAKED WHITEBAIT

8 servings

- *250 grams dried bread crumbs*
- *2 cloves finely chopped garlic, green shoots removed*
- *3 chilli peppers, finely chopped*
- *finely chopped parsley*
- *olive oil*
- *1 kilo whitebait (marides)*
- *salt, freshly ground pepper*

*P*reheat the oven to 200 °C. Mix the breadcrumbs with the chopped garlic, chillis and parsley. Season with salt and pepper to taste.

Oil a baking dish and sprinkle it with a handful of the breadcrumb mixture.

Clean the fish and remove their heads, pulling out the backbone at the same time. Make a slit down the middle, and separate the two fillets. Lay the fish on the oiled baking dish, fillet side up, with their tails pointing toward the centre. Make one or more concentric circles with the larger fish on the outside and the smaller ones on the inside. Sprinkle the fish with the rest of the breadcrumb mixture. Arrange the remaining fish in the same way on top of the first layer, this time skin side up. Sprinkle with a little olive oil.

Bake for about 15 minutes.

The Greek *marida* is not quite equivalent to the Atlantic whitebait, being a bit larger. You could also use fresh anchovies or smelts in this dish.

BOURDETTO

This is a variation on the traditional Corfiot dish. The fish called for here is a type of grouper, but any firm, white-fleshed fish will do.

4-5 servings

- *1 1/2 kilos sfirida or other white fish, sliced*
- *juice of 1 1/2 lemons*
- *extra virgin olive oil*
- *3 garlic cloves, halved, green shoots removed*
- *thyme*
- *salt, freshly ground pepper*

Wash the fish, arrange the slices on a platter, sprinkle with lemon juice and salt and pepper and leave to marinate for a good hour.

In a wide saucepan sauté the garlic in 6-7 tablespoons of oil over medium-low heat for 30 seconds. Remove the garlic with a slotted spoon and add the fish slices and their juices from the platter. Add more salt and pepper to taste, cover, lower the heat and simmer for 12-15 minutes, depending on the thickness of the fish. Sprinkle with a little thyme, simmer for 1-2 minutes more and serve.

*S*EA BREAM WITH CELERY

4 servings

- *4-6 open-sea gilt - head or other bream*
- *600 grams celery*
- *juice of 2 lemons*
- *1/2 teaspoon arrowroot*
- *salt, freshly ground pepper*

*W*ash the fish and sprinkle them with salt and pepper and the juice of one lemon. Let stand for an hour or so on a rack to absorb the flavours.

Cut the celery into rounds about 4 cm long and parboil them in 500 ml (2 cups) of lightly salted water for 3-4 minutes. Place the fish on top of the celery, dust with arrowroot, shake the pan to distribute the thickener, bring to a boil and after 1-2 minutes, cover and cook for 12-14 minutes. Add the juice of the second lemon, stirring gently, sprinkle with lots of pepper, boil for another 2 minutes and serve.

ROAST POUSSIN CORFIOT STYLE

2 servings

- *1 poussin*
- *2 leeks, finely chopped*
- *8 tablespoons tangerine liqueur*
- *300 grams kumquats*
- *4-5 tablespoons extra virgin olive oil*
- *100 ml brandy*
- *250 ml hot chicken broth*
- *salt and freshly ground pepper*

Preheat the oven to 200 °C. Wash and dry the poussin, fill the cavity with half the chopped leek and 2 tablespoons tangerine liqueur, season with salt and pepper.

Cut the kumquats in two, remove the seeds and stuff the poussin with half of them. Truss the poussin with kitchen string.

Gently heat the oil in an ovenproof saucepan and sauté the second leek until it softens and starts to smell good. Raise the heat, add the poussin and brown it on all sides. Pour in the brandy and before it evaporates completely, add the hot broth and boil for 5 minutes. Add the rest of the kumquats and 6 tablespoons of tangerine liqueur. Cover the saucepan and bake in the oven for 30 minutes.

Turn off the oven and let the poussin rest in it for 10 minutes before serving.

STEWING CHICKEN MILANESE STYLE

4 servings

- 1 free-range hen or chicken, 1,700-1,800 grams
- 1/2 lemon
- 2 carrots, halved lengthwise
- 1 onion, halved, and studded with
- 3 cloves
- 110 grams butter
- 80 grams Carolina rice
- 60 grams flour
- 200 ml milk
- 2 egg yolks
- nutmeg
- salt, freshly ground pepper
- 60 grams grated Parmesan

Wash the hen well, rub it all over with half a lemon, let dry and truss. Boil 2 litres of water with the carrots and clove-studded onion for 10 minutes and add the hen and salt and pepper. Skim off all the froth and simmer for about 1 hour, until tender. Remove the hen from the pot.

Melt 20 grams of butter over medium heat, add the rice and stir until it becomes opaque (about 2 minutes), add 80 ml of the chicken broth, pepper, and bring to the boil. Cover and cook for 15-18 minutes.

Debone the hen and place the meat on the boiled rice. Cover with a clean tea towel and set aside for 10 minutes.

Melt 30 grams of butter and stir it into the chicken and rice to warm it up.

Melt the remaining butter over medium heat, add the flour and stir with a wooden spoon until there are no lumps and the flour is golden brown. Off the stove, add the milk and about 3 cups of chicken broth, stirring constantly. Lower the heat, return the pan to the stove, and stir until you have a thin béchamel sauce. Remove from the heat, add a few gratings of nutmeg, pepper and the egg yolks. Stir until the yolks are absorbed. Add 30 grams of Parmesan, return to the stove, and warm for 1-2 minutes. Mix the pilaf and the chicken meat with the sauce. Spoon the contents of the pot into a large ring mould and unmould it onto a serving dish. Sprinkle with the rest of the grated cheese.

$\mathcal{Q}$UAIL WITH CHERRIES

4 servings

- *300 grams dried cherries*
- *200 ml grappa or brandy*
- *4 quail*
- *1 lemon*
- *5-6 tablespoons olive oil*
- *salt, freshly ground pepper*

$\mathcal{R}$inse the cherries. Heat 1/2 cup of water, add the grappa, throw in the cherries, cover and set aside for a few hours until they soften and swell up.

Wash, pick over and dry the quail, rub their breast cavity with lemon juice and salt and pepper, and truss with kitchen string.

Brown the birds in 2-3 tablespoons of oil over medium-high heat until their skins turn a deep gold. Remove the quail with a slotted spoon and drain them on paper towels. Pour away the cooking oil, wipe the pan and add 3 tablespoons of new oil. Turn the heat to medium and as soon as the oil starts to smoke, replace the birds.

Remove the cherries from the grappa, add the alcohol to the pan with the quail, bring to a boil, cover and simmer for 15 minutes.

Add the cherries, and salt and pepper to taste, cover and cook for 10-12 minutes. When the birds are fork tender, remove from the stove and let rest a few minutes before serving.

You can serve the birds filleted or whole.

*E*XOTIC MEATBALLS

50 little balls

- *55 grams sesame seeds*
- *cumin to taste, optional*
- *350 grams ground lamb (from the leg)*
- *150 grams ground pork*
- *1 egg*
- *1 chilli pepper, finely chopped*
- *cinnamon to taste, optional*
- *finely chopped mint, to taste*
- *finely chopped fresh coriander, to taste*
- *salt*
- *sesame seed oil for frying*
- *cornflour*

*B*rown the sesame seeds in a non-stick frying pan until they start to pop. Brown the cumin separately until it starts to release its fragrance. Mix all the ingredients together, except for half the sesame seeds. Cover and refrigerate for at least 2 hours.

Break off bits of the meat mixture and roll into little balls. Dust with cornflour and the extra sesame seeds. Heat the sesame oil in a non-stick frying pan, over medium-low heat, and fry the meatballs a few at a time for 3-4 minutes until they are golden brown. Drain on absorbent paper and serve with hearts of lettuce.

*M*EAT PATTIES WITH PISTACHIO NUTS

4 servings

- *400 grams ground lamb*
- *200 grams dried breadcrumbs*
- *2 hot chillis, finely chopped*
- *4 tablespoons olive oil plus some extra*
- *2 medium onions, grated*
- *60 grams shelled pistachios, coarsely chopped*
- *salt, freshly ground pepper*

Combine the mincemeat with 120 grams of the breadcrumbs, the chillis, salt and pepper.

Gently heat the oil in a heavy saucepan and brown the onions until they start to caramelize. Season with salt and pepper, add 80 grams of breadcrumbs and the pistachios.

Shape the mincemeat into 8 oval patties. Divide the pistachio mixture into 8 equal portions, make a hollow in each pattie and press in the pistachios. Reshape the patties, brush with a little oil and grill them in the oven or over charcoal outdoors.

ELENITSA'S SOUTZOUKAKIA

These cumin-flavoured meatballs are a speciality from the former Greek city of Smyrna, present day Izmir, in what is now Turkey.

4-5 servings

- *150 grams yesterday's Greek or Italian country bread*
- *200 ml Mavrodaphne or other sweet red wine*
- *300 grams ground lean pork*
- *400 grams ground lamb, from the leg*
- *2 eggs, beaten*
- *1 teaspoon cumin, heated in a saucepan*
- *cinnamon*
- *4-5 tablespoons olive oil for frying*
- *salt, freshly ground pepper*

the sauce

- *3 tablespoons olive oil*
- *1 garlic clove, green shoot removed*
- *600 grams ripe tomatoes, peeled and chopped*
- *cinnamon*
- *2 cloves*
- *300 ml chicken or vegetable broth*
- *salt, freshly ground pepper*

Soak the bread in the wine and as soon as it has softened, remove it and squeeze all the liquid out. In a bowl mix the mincemeat thoroughly with the bread, eggs, and spices. Cover and let the flavours mingle for several hours or even overnight in the refrigerator.

Break off piece of the meat and shape them into oval patties, about 6 cm long and 3 cm wide.

Heat the oil to smoking in a non-stick frying pan and fry the meatballs a few at a time until they are a deep brown all over. Drain both sides on paper towels.

To make the sauce, sauté the garlic in a deep non-stick saucepan for 30 seconds in the olive oil. Remove it with a slotted spoon and discard. Add the tomatoes and seasonings and sauté for about 10 minutes. Add the broth, bring to a boil and boil for 3-4 minutes. Add the meatballs, stir and simmer for another 10 minutes, uncovered. Serve with fried potatoes or rice.

$\mathcal{L}$OU'S VEAL WITH QUINCES

4 servings

- *1 kilo veal or young beef*
- *1 kilo quinces*
- *4-5 tablespoons olive oil*
- *2 cinnamon sticks*
- *1 1/2 litres chicken broth*
- *2-3 tablespoons honey, thyme-flavoured if possible*
- *salt, freshly ground pepper*

Ask the butcher to cut you 5-6 pieces of beef or veal for stewing. Wash, drain and dry the meat.

Cut the quinces vertically in slices, peel and place in a bowl of water to prevent discoloration.

Brown the meat on all sides in moderately hot oil until it is a deep golden brown. Season with salt and pepper, add the cinnamon and broth and bring to a boil, cover, lower the heat and simmer for 20-25 minutes.

Remove the meat from the pot with a slotted spoon and set aside. Add the quinces and honey to the broth, stir, add salt and pepper to taste and boil for 15 minutes.

Return the meat to the pot, stir and cook for another 10 minutes. Place the meat and fruit on a serving platter, and boil the broth/sauce over high heat for a few minutes to reduce by at least half. Pour the sauce over the dish and serve.

SPICY ROAST KID OR LAMB WITH CUMIN

4 servings

- *2 tablespoons cumin*
- *5 garlic cloves*
- *1 chilli pepper cut in rings*
- *extra virgin olive oil*
- *1 tablespoon thyme*
- *leg of spring lamb or kid*
- *salt, freshly ground pepper*

Preheat the oven to 150 °C. Heat a non-stick frying pan and when it starts to smoke, add the cumin and brown until it darkens and releases its aroma.

Peel the garlic cloves, leaving the last layer intact, and place them on a piece of aluminium foil along with the chilli pepper. Sprinkle with a little oil and salt, seal the foil, and bake for 15 minutes. Lower the heat to 100 °C and bake for another 40 minutes. Purée the garlic cream, chilli pepper, cumin, thyme and salt in a small mixer.

Wash and dry the meat and make small gashes in the flesh with a sharp knife. Fill the little pockets with the aromatic mixture and spread any left over on the surface of the meat. If you wish, you can also triple the amount of seasonings and cover the whole leg with the purée. Cover and refrigerate overnight.

Preheat the oven to 220 °C. Oil a roasting pan and sprinkle oil on the meat as well. Bake for 15 minutes. Turn the meat, lower the heat to 150 °C and bake for another 2 1/2 hours or until the meat is extremely tender. Turn off the oven, open the door and let the kid or lamb rest for 10 minutes. Serve with a mixed salad.

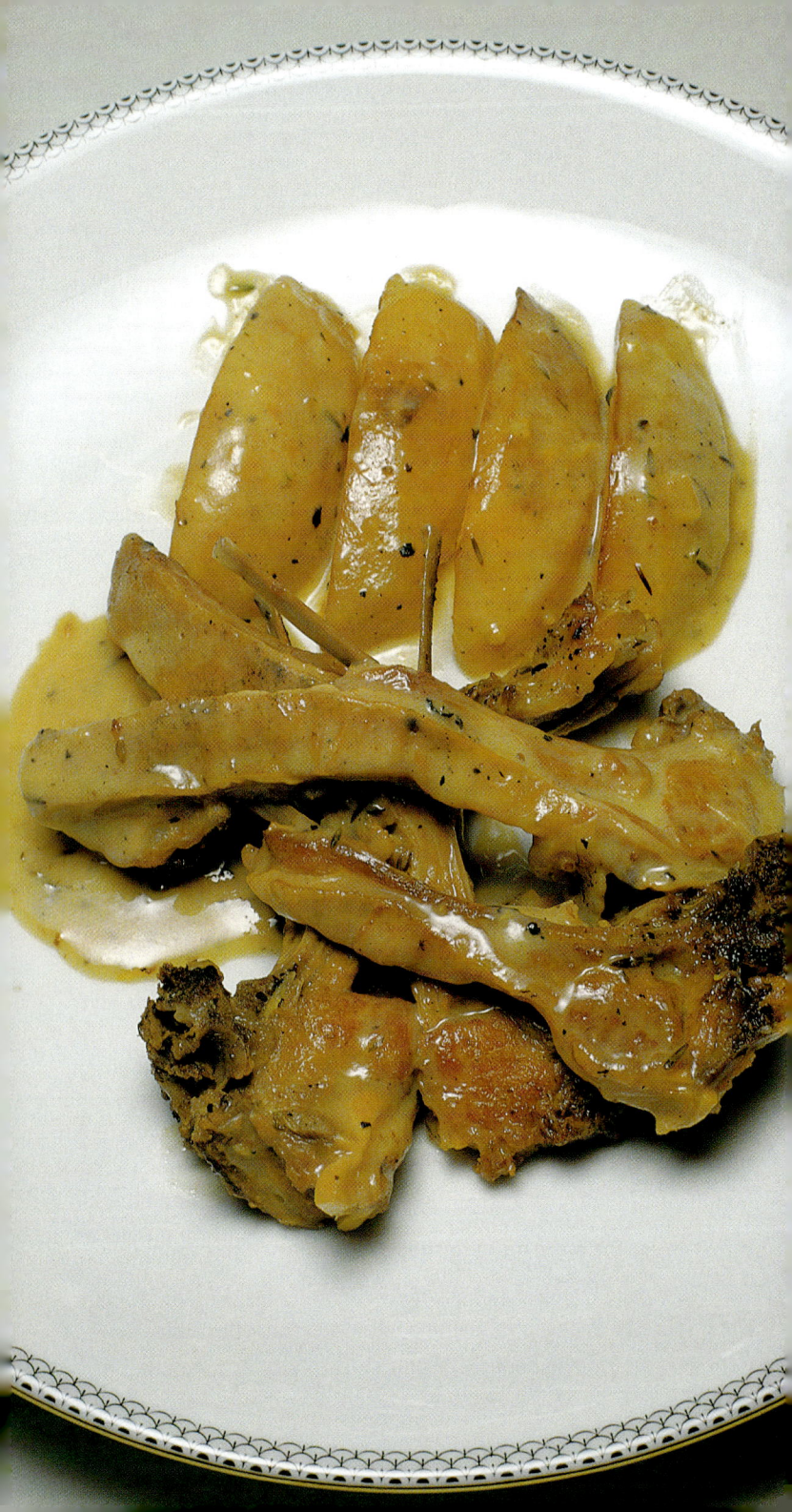

KID WITH EGG-LEMON SAUCE FROM HYDRA

- *800 grams boneless spring lamb or kid, cut in large cubes*
- *extra virgin olive oil*
- *a sprig of rosemary*
- *rind and juice of 1 1/2 lemons plus lemon juice for soaking the potatoes*
- *1 kilo small new potatoes, of equal size*
- *2 eggs*
- *salt, freshly ground pepper*

Wash and dry the meat. Place it in a bowl with a little oil, rosemary, pepper, lemon rind and marinate for at least 2 hours or overnight in the refrigerator. Peel and cube the potatoes. Soak the potatoes in water and a little lemon juice.

Heat 4 tablespoons of oil in a large non-stick saucepan and brown the meat over a high heat. Add 1 cup of water, salt, lower the heat to medium, cover and simmer for 20-25 minutes.

Heat 4-5 tablespoons of oil in a non-stick frying pan and brown the potatoes over medium heat for 3-4 minutes. Drain and place the potatoes in the saucepan with the meat, season and simmer for 15 minutes.

Beat the eggs with 2 tablespoons of water. Slowly add 2-3 tablespoons of the juices from the meat to the eggs, and beat until thoroughly blended. Add the lemon juice, continue to beat, and off the stove add the egg-lemon sauce to the stewpot, stirring constantly and shaking the pan. Warm gently for 2-3 minutes, taste, add pepper and serve.

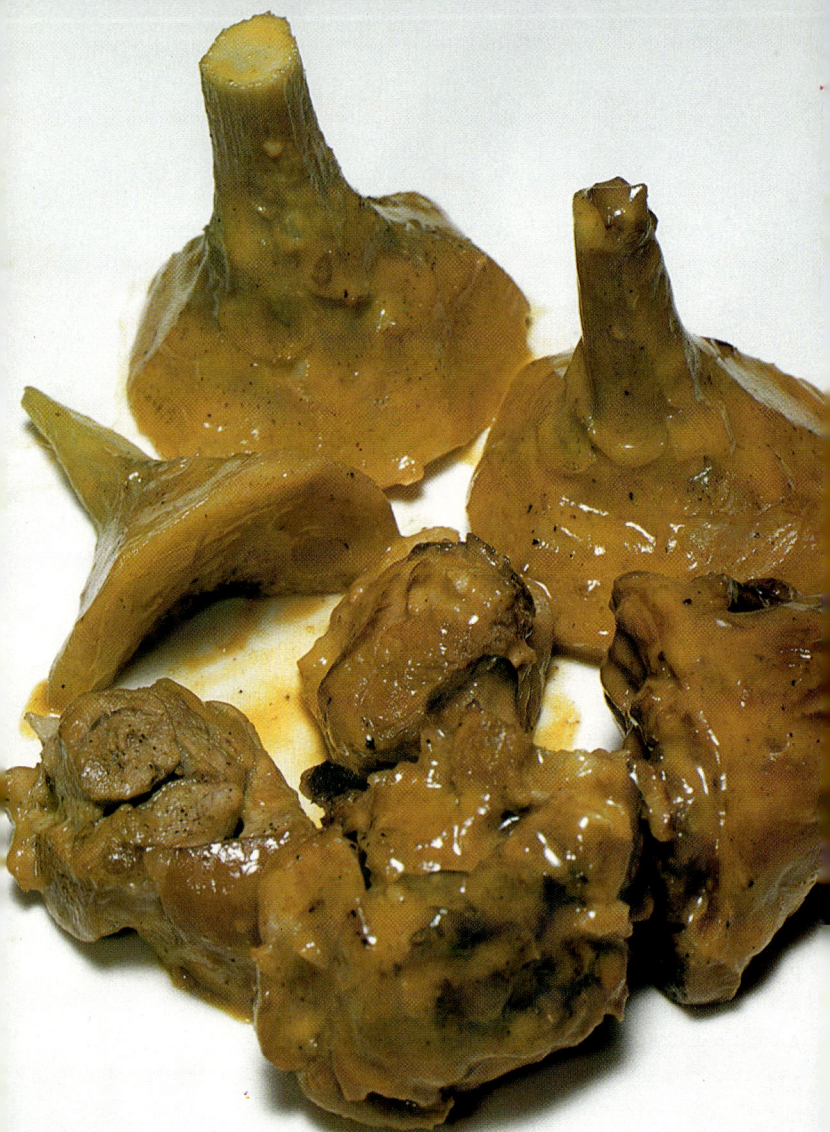

KID WITH ARTICHOKES AND EGG-LEMON SAUCE

4 servings

- *700 grams lean boned kid or spring lamb (from the leg and shoulder), bones reserved*
- *8 artichokes*
- *juice of 2 lemons plus 1 lemon, sliced, and grated rind of 1 lemon*
- *4-5 tablespoons extra virgin olive oil*
- *1 medium onion, grated*
- *4 spring onions, finely chopped*
- *300 ml homemade meat broth*
- *salt, freshly ground pepper to taste*
- *1 egg plus 1 yolk*
- *a pinch of cornflour (for the inexperienced)*

Ask the butcher to break the bones. Roast them in a hot oven for 40 minutes and then boil them with vegetables to produce 1/3 litre broth.

Wash and dry the meat and cut into bite-sized pieces.

Clean the artichokes, placing them in a bowl with water and the lemon slices so they don't discolour. Slice each artichoke heart in half.

Pour the oil into a flat saucepan and over medium heat sauté the grated onion until soft for 5 minutes. Add the spring onions and wilt for 3-4 minutes. Add the meat, raising the heat, and brown it until the cubes become a rich gold. Add the hot broth and as soon as it comes back to the boil, lower the heat to medium, cover, and simmer for 15 to 20 minutes. Add the artichokes, juice and rind of 1 lemon, salt and pepper, cover again and simmer until the artichokes and the meat are very tender.

With a fork beat the egg, yolk, lemon juice and cornflour, if you're using it, in a second saucepan. Add the broth from meat/artichokes to the mixture little by little, stirring constantly. When you have added all the broth, simmer the sauce for 3-4 minutes. Pour the egg-lemon sauce over the meat, shaking the pan to mix it thoroughly, and serve.

$\mathscr{B}$ABY LAMB OR KID WITH WILD FENNEL

4 servings

- *1 kilo spring lamb or kid*
- *olive oil*
- *4 spring onions*
- *2 tomatoes, grated, skins discarded*
- *1 cup wild fennel or bulb fennel leaves, finely chopped*
- *salt, freshly ground pepper*

$\mathcal{W}$ash and dry the meat and cut it into serving portions. Gently heat the oil in a saucepan and brown the spring onions for 2-4 minutes until they become translucent and start to release their aroma. Raise the heat and brown the meat on all sides until it is golden brown. Add the tomatoes and fennel, bring to a boil and immediately lower the heat, cover and simmer for 30 minutes. Season with salt and pepper, re-cover and simmer until the meat is very tender. Serve immediately.

*H*ARE WITH PISTACHIOS

6 servings

- *1 hare, 1,500-1,800 grams, cut in serving portions (frozen hare filets can also be used)*
- *2-3 garlic cloves, green shoots removed*
- *140 grams pistachio nuts, coarsely chopped*
- *9 tablespoons olive oil*
- *200 ml dry white wine*
- *300 ml chicken broth*
- *salt, coarsely ground pepper*

Wash and dry the hare. If using fresh hare, reserve the liver. Preheat the oven to 200 °C. Mash the garlic with 2/3 teaspoon salt, add 80 grams of pistachios, 4 tablespoons oil and pepper, continue mashing into a paste. With a sharp knife make slashes in the meat and fill them with the pistachio mixture. Rub the rest of the paste into the meat.

In an ovenproof casserole sauté the hare in 5 tablespoons of hot oil until all sides are golden brown. Pour in the wine and with a wooden spoon scrape up any bits of meat from the sides and bottom of the pan. Add salt and pepper to taste along with the broth and bring to a boil. Cover the pot and bake for 35 minutes.

Remove the meat from the oven, add the remaining pistachios, replace the lid and bake for another 15-20 minutes until the hare is tender.

In a non-stick frying pan fry the liver in 1 tablespoon of oil, chop it and add it to the sauce. If the sauce appears too thin, boil it vigorously until reduced.

CAKE FOR SAINT FANOURIOS

St. Fanourios is the Greek equivalent of St. Anthony, the finder of lost things and people. On his day, August 27th, many Greek housewives prepare a cake in his honour.

- *250 grams self-raising flour*
- *100 grams sugar*
- *60 grams walnuts, coarsely chopped*
- *30 grams sultanas*
- *cinnamon powder*
- *1 cup extra virgin olive oil*
- *250 ml orange juice and grated rind of 1 orange*
- *75 ml lemon juice and grated rind of 1 lemon*
- *75 ml brandy*

Preheat the oven to 180 °C. Mix all the solid ingredients in a large bowl, add the liquids and stir into a thick batter, adding a little water if necessary.

Oil a cake pan, dust it with flour and empty the batter into the pan and bake for 25-35 minutes.

*R*OSE - PETAL SORBET

4-6 servings

- *220 grams rose-flavoured sugar*
- *juice and rind of 1 lemon*
- *4 man-sized handfuls of rose petals*
- *a few drops of glycerine*

*A*dd the sugar to 2 cups of water (480 ml), bring to a boil and boil vigorously for 3-4 minutes.

Set the syrup aside to cool and add the lemon rind and rose petals, pressing down with a wooden spoon to moisten them well. Cover the mixture with cellophane wrap and refrigerate all night.

Strain the flavoured syrup which should have acquired a dark yellow, rather unappetizing colour. Add a few drops of glycerine, up to 1 teaspoonful, and the lemon juice. This will turn the syrup a deep pink.

Raise the thermostat in your freezer to maximum, pour the syrup into a metal container, and freeze for 1 hour. Remove from the freezer and beat the sorbet with a wire whisk, pressing the crystals away from the sides and bottom of the container towards the centre. Refreeze for 40 minutes. Repeat the procedure another 2-3 times every half hour until the sorbet is light and crystal-free. Return the thermostat to normal and leave the sorbet in the freezer until 30 minutes before you wish to serve it.

Divide the sorbet among 4-6 glasses and serve.

𝒫URPLE SORBET

- *500 ml juice of blood oranges*
- *peel from 3 of the reddest oranges*
- *100 grams sugar*
- *6-7 tablespoons tsipouro or grappa or vodka*

Cut the orange peel into matchstick-thin strips and boil for 3 minutes in a little water to remove their bitterness. Drain, put them in a saucepan with 125 ml water (1 1/2 cups) and the sugar, and boil until half the water has evaporated. Set the syrup aside to cool.

Mix the juice and alcohol with the syrup and pour it into a metal container. Freeze for 80 minutes until crystals form on the sides of the container. Stir with a wire whisk, scraping the crystals into the still liquid centre of the container. Freeze for another 30-40 minutes, whisk again, and repeat the procedure twice more at half hour intervals.

This recipe will be far easier to execute with an ice cream maker.

PISTACHIO ICE CREAM

6 servings

- *70 grams shelled pistachios*
- *105 grams sugar*
- *600 ml milk*
- *7 egg yolks*

Raise the thermostat in your freezer to maximum. Blend the pistachios with 30 grams of sugar until they are finely ground. Boil the mixture in 100 ml of milk for 3 minutes. Cover and set aside to cool.

Beat the egg yolks with 75 grams of sugar in the mixer until they are pale yellow and smooth. Bring 500 ml of milk to a boil and trickle it into the egg yolk mixture, stirring constantly with a wooden spoon. Transfer the mixture to a saucepan and simmer for 1 minute, stirring all the while.

Remove the pan from the heat and pour the liquid through a fine strainer into a metal container. Add the pistachios to the liquid and freeze for 45 minutes until fragile crystals appear on the sides of the container.

Beat the ice cream with a wire whisk, pushing the crystals toward the still soft centre. Repeat this procedure every 30 minutes until the ice cream is firm. Reset the thermostat to normal. Remove the ice cream from the freezer 20 minutes before serving.

CINNAMON ICE CREAM WITH APPLES

- litre milk
- 20 grams salep*, optional
- 20 grams sugar
- 2 cinnamon sticks
- 400 grams Granny Smith apples, peeled and cored
- 30 grams butter
- powdered cinnamon
- 4 tablespoons finely chopped ginger
- 1/2 nutmeg, grated
- freshly ground pepper
- 5 tablespoons grappa or vodka

*D*issolve the salep or cornflour in 240 ml (cup) of milk. Bring the remaining milk to a boil with 90 grams of sugar and the cinnamon sticks and simmer for 4-5 minutes. Remove from the heat and pour a little of the hot milk into the cold milk, stirring constantly with a wire whisk. Gradually add the rest of the boiled milk, stirring, and over low heat add the ginger, nutmeg and pepper. Simmer for a few minutes until it starts to thicken. Set in the refrigerator to cool and freeze in an ice cream maker according to the manufacturer's instructions. Place the resulting ice cream in the freezer.

Cut the apples into cubes, melt the butter in a non-stick frying pan and sauté them over moderate heat. Preheat the grill. Dust the apples with 30 grams of sugar and place under the grill to caramelize. Douse with the alcohol and set alight with a long match. Sprinkle with cinnamon and serve along with the ice cream.

Don't forget to take the ice cream out of the freezer 20-30 minutes before serving.

Salep is a spice made from ground orchid bulbs. It is used in the Middle East to flavour a winter drink that used to be sold in Greece as well by street vendors. Use cornflour if you cannot get hold of it.

$\mathcal{M}$RS. HARITOULA'S CUSTARD PIE

for a large pie

- *1 1/2 liters milk plus a little more for glazing the top*
- *125 grams butter plus a little extra*
- *60 grams sugar*
- *pinch of salt*
- *110 grams semolina*
- *8 fresh laid eggs plus 1 for glazing the top*

$\mathcal{B}$oil the milk together with the butter, sugar and salt. Add the semolina, stirring constantly with a wooden spoon until the mixture thickens. Set aside to cool.

Preheat the oven to 200 °C.

Butter a non-stick baking dish.

Add the eggs, one at a time, to the cooled custard, whisking all the while. Pour the custard into the baking dish.

Beat the extra egg with 2-3 tablespoons milk and paint the surface of the custard with it.

Set the dish on the middle rack of the oven and bake for 45 minutes or bake for 5 minutes on the oven floor and then raise it to the middle.

DIPLES

These feather-light fried pastry bows and squares are a traditional treat over the New Year.

- 500 grams fine semolina
- 1/2 teaspoon baking soda or baking powder
- 2 pinches salt
- juice of 2 oranges
- juice of 1 lemon
- 8 eggs
- honey, coarsely chopped walnuts
- oil for frying

Mix the semolina, soda and salt with the citrus juices and the eggs in a medium-sized bowl.

Using your hands or the pastry attachment on your mixer, work the mixture into a thick dough. Roll out the dough with a rolling pin, sprinkling a little water over it if needed, to make it more manageable. Break off smaller pieces of the dough and roll out into parallelograms about 1/2 cm thick and cut with a pastry wheel or a wet knife. You can also twist them into bows.

Heat the oil in a deep pan to medium hot and fry the diples quickly, a few at a time, until they are light gold on both sides. Remove from the oil with a slotted spoon and drain on paper towels.

Pile the pastries on a platter and sprinkle with honey and chopped nuts.

*B*ERGAMOT-FLAVOURED RICE PUDDING

6 servings

- *1 1/2 litres milk*
- *40 grams sugar, optional*
- *300 grams short-grain rice*
- *70 grams butter*
- *150 ml sweet Samos wine or sherry*
- *70 grams glazed bergamot, finely chopped*
- *2 tablespoons rose water*
- *freshly ground black pepper*

*M*ix the sugar with the milk, if you want a sweeter pudding. Bring the milk to the boil and keep it hot on a low burner. Sauté the rice in 40 grams of melted butter over medium-low heat for 3-4 minutes, until it turns golden.

Raise the heat and pour in the wine. As soon as the wine has evaporated, add 2 tablespoons of hot milk, stirring with a wooden spoon until the milk is absorbed. Add 2 more tablespoons of milk and stir.

Continue in this way, making sure the rice does not stick, and when you get to the last of the milk, pour it in and remove the pan from the heat. Add the bergamot, 30 grams of butter, rose water and stir. Return the pan to the burner for one minute, sprinkle with a lot of pepper, cover and remove from the stove.

Let the rice pudding stand for 5 minutes. Divide it into 6 deep soup or consommé bowls and refrigerate for a while.

This pudding can also be served warm.

NIKI'S MOCHA CREAM

- *250 grams butter at room temperature*
- *80 grams confectioners sugar*
- *3 tablespoons coffee liqueur*
- *1 1/2 cups strong Greek coffee (or espresso)*
- *a few coffee beans, coarsely ground*
- *60 grams almonds, browned and coarsely chopped*

Beat the butter in the mixer at medium speed until it is light and fluffy. Add the sugar slowly while continuing to beat. Add the liqueur and the coffee a little at a time. Empty the mixture into a pastry horn and squeeze it into serving bowls. Garnish with the crushed almonds and coffee beans.

Halvas

This is a quick and easy dessert that is a favourite staple in Greek tavernas, usually offered on the house.

8-10 servings

- *2 cups water*
- *2 cups sugar*
- *rind of 1 lemon*
- *3 cinnamon sticks*
- *3 cups milk*
- *1 cup butter*
- *2 cups coarse semolina*
- *1/2 cup almonds, coarsely chopped*
- *powdered cinnamon*

Boil the water with the sugar, lemon peel and cinnamon sticks for 3 minutes. Add the milk, boil for 1-2 minutes, taking care that it doesn't boil over. Remove from the stove and cover to keep warm.

Heat the butter in a wide saucepan until it starts to burn, gradually add the semolina, stirring with a wooden spoon until it turns a dark gold. Add the chopped almonds and brown them, too, continuing to stir. Remove the pan from the heat and pour in the milk mixture all at once. Lower the heat, return to the stove and simmer until the halvas thickens. Remove the cinnamon sticks, remove the pan from the stove and cover it with a tea towel for 5 minutes. Sprinkle cinnamon over the surface, stir and spoon the halvas into a mould, pressing down with a spoon to remove air bubbles. Leave the halvas in the mould to cool a bit and then demould it on the serving dish.

ℛOSE-PETAL RISOTTO

6 servings

- *80 grams rose petals from the garden*
- *350 grams rose-flavoured sugar*
- *300 grams short-grain rice*
- *80 grams butter*
- *200 ml sweet Samos wine or sherry*
- *freshly ground pepper*

Carefully wash the rose petals. Boil 1 litre of water with the sugar for 4-5 minutes and set the syrup aside to cool. When it is tepid, add the rose petals, pressing them down with a wooden spoon to moisten them thoroughly. Cover with cling film and refrigerate overnight or for at least 6 hours. Drain, reserving the aromatic syrup. Heat gently without boiling.

Sauté the rice in 50 grams of melted butter over medium-high heat for 3-5 minutes, stirring all the while until the rice is translucent and starts to pop. Pour in the wine and when most of it has evaporated, add 1-2 tablespoons of the syrup. Stir and as soon as the liquid has been absorbed, add another 1-2 tablespoons of syrup. Stir and repeat the procedure 2-3 times until the rice has the smooth texture of risotto and has that al dente texture (not soft). Remove from the heat, stir in the remaining butter, cover and let rest for 5 minutes before serving, sprinkled with lots of freshly ground black pepper.

WALNUT CAKE

for a medium-sized cake

- *4 cups of shelled walnuts, coarsely chopped*
- *250 grams vanilla-flavoured self-raising flour*
- *1 teaspoon ground cinnamon*
- *4 tablespoons butter at room temperature plus extra*
- *200 grams sugar*
- *8 eggs, separated*
- *dry breadcrumbs*
- *15 ml brandy*

Preheat the oven to 200 °C. Mix the flour with the cinnamon and 3 cups of the walnuts.

Beat the butter in a small mixer until it becomes white and fluffy. Add the sugar and the butter to the mixer's large bowl and beat at medium speed until fluffy. Add the egg yolks, one at a time. Beat the whites until peaks form.

Add the egg whites and the flour to the butter, alternately, in three doses. Butter a non-stick cake pan and coat it with the breadcrumbs. Pour the batter into the pan and sprinkle with the remaining walnuts. Bake for 45-50 minutes or until the cake passes the knife test, ie a sharp knife inserted into it comes out dry. Let cool 10 minutes. Remove to the serving dish and sprinkle with the brandy.

*M*ASTIC-FLAVOURED MERINGUES

24 pieces

- *4 grams Chios mastic*
- *170 grams confectioners sugar*
- *grated rind of 1 lemon*
- *whites of 4 large eggs*
- *20 grams butter*
- *a little flour*
- *30 grams sugar*

*C*arefully wash and dry the mixer bowl. Preheat the oven to 140 °C. Pound the mastic crystals to a fine powder and combine with the confectioners sugar and lemon rind. In the mixer beat the egg whites until they become firm. Add 2 tablespoons of confectioners sugar, continuing to beat for 1-2 minutes. Add the remaining confectioners sugar, sprinkling the powder over the bowl while working the mixer, until the meringue glistens and holds its shape. Empty the meringue into the cleanest possible pastry horn.

Lightly butter a large, clean baking sheet and sprinkle it with a little flour. Use the pastry horn to squeeze out 24 egg-shaped meringues, sprinkle them with sugar and let them stand 10 minutes to absorb the sugar. Bake for 15 minutes, lower the oven to 120 °C and bake for another 45-60 minutes. The meringues should be as white as milk with only the sugar crystals tinted gold in contrast to the surface as a whole.

Remove the baking sheet from the oven and gently unstick the meringues, turn them upside down and bake for 5-6 minutes to make sure their insides dry.

Serve with kaimaki ice cream, if you can find it, or the ice cream of your choice.

Mastic is the crystallized resin of a tree found only in southern Chios and because of its gummy texture was highly prized as the first chewing gum. Kaimaki ice cream is also made with mastic, giving it a taste quite distinct from vanilla. If mastic is not available, use a few drops of vanilla extract in the meringues.

$\mathcal{F}$LOWER-SCENTED SUGAR

for 3 jars

- *50 grams rose petals*
- *50 grams jasmine petals*
- *3 tablespoons lavender flowers*
- *3 vanilla beans*
- *3 cups (250 grams each) sugar*

$\mathcal{C}$arefully wash each type of flower separately. Spread out the blossoms on towels and let them dry completely. Slit each vanilla bean lengthwise with a sharp knife and open the pods.

Pour the sugar into 3 glass jars or metal containers which can be hermetically sealed.

Scrape the vanilla seeds from one pod into each of the 3 jars.

Put the rose petals in the first jar, the jasmine in the second and the lavender in the third. Mix thoroughly with a wooden spoon, close the jars and leave untouched for 10 to 15 days. Remove the flowers and use the sugar in cakes and custards.

$\mathcal{S}$OUMADA - TRADITIONAL ALMOND SQUASH

- *280 grams blanched almonds*
- *850 ml hot water*
- *1 kilo sugar*
- *2 tablespoons bitter almond liqueur*
- *a few drops of bitter almond extract*

$\mathcal{F}$inely grind the almonds in the mixer. Empty the ground almonds into a colander lined with a piece of doubled cheesecloth above a bowl. Little by little pour half the hot water over them, close the cloth and squeeze it so that the water will permeate the almonds. Open the cloth and pour the remaining water over the ground almonds, close and squeeze again, as tight as you can.
Boil the almond juice with the sugar for 8 minutes. Set aside to cool, add the liqueur and almond extract and store in sterilized bottles.

Serve the soumada diluted with carbonated mineral water. It is very refreshing on a hot summer's day and was traditionally drunk at weddings on some islands.

Notes